7
Creation Miracles
of Christ
BRAD FORLOW

INSTITUTE
for CREATION
RESEARCH

Dallas, Texas
www.icr.org

7 Creation Miracles of Christ

by Brad Forlow, Ph.D.

All Scripture quotations are from the New King James Version.

ISBN: 978-1-935587-10-1

Please visit our website for other books and resources: www.icr.org

Printed in the United States of America.

TABLE OF CONTENTS

INTRODUCTION

No star. No angels. No shepherds. No wise men. No mention of Bethlehem or Mary and Joseph. No compelling story of the babe in a manger. No genealogy of Jesus to introduce His birth. No elaborate "Christmas story" describing the events preceding and surrounding the birth of Jesus.

John the apostle does none of these things when he begins to tell the story of Jesus of Nazareth.

Instead, he pens a unique introduction to the words and works of Jesus that reaches back to eternity past, echoing the introductory phrase in Genesis—"in the beginning." John establishes the nature and character of Jesus as he begins to unfold such familiar themes as life and light to describe the One who became flesh and lived among us.

Why are there four different gospels? How different are they? Do they contradict one another? Why did God inspire four accounts of Jesus' story?

Although all four gospels record the life, ministry, death, and resurrection of Jesus, each is distinct, written from the author's own perspective. Each author is writing to a specific audience for a specific purpose. From the pages of each gospel emerges a unique, but complementary, portrait of Jesus Christ.

Matthew presents Jesus as the Messiah to his Jewish audience. Mark offers a call to discipleship where Jesus is Lord desiring a fruitful, right relationship and proper worship from His people. Luke emphasizes Jesus as teacher and seeks to make the Gentiles certain of the things that Jesus has taught. But John's purpose in writing is clearly defined by John himself—Jesus is the Christ, the Son of God, and the source of eternal life.

> And truly Jesus did many other signs in the presence of His disciples, which are not written in this book; but these are written that you may believe that Jesus is the Christ, the Son of God, and that believing you may have life in His name. (John 20:30-31)

John begins by stating and developing the "thesis" that he will defend as he tells Jesus' story. He describes the nature and character of Jesus, boldly declaring who this Person is. And while he recounts the earthly ministry of Jesus, John does not focus on His humanity, as the other gospel writers do, but rather on His deity.

> In the beginning was the Word, and the Word was with God, and the Word was God. He was in the beginning with God. All things were made through Him, and without Him nothing was made that was made. In Him was life, and the life was the light of men. And the light shines in the darkness, and the darkness did not comprehend it. There was a man sent from God, whose name was John. This man came for a witness, to bear witness of the Light, that all through him might believe. He was not that Light, but was sent to bear witness of that Light. That was the true Light which gives light to every man coming into the world. He was in the world, and the world was made through Him, and the world did not know Him. He came to His own, and His own did not receive Him. But as many as received Him, to them He gave the right to become children of God, to those who believe in His name: who were born, not of blood, nor of the will of the flesh, nor of the will of man, but of God. And the Word became flesh and dwelt among us, and we beheld His glory, the glory as of the only begotten of the Father, full of grace and truth. John bore witness of Him and cried out, saying, "This was He of whom I said, 'He who comes after me is preferred before me, for He was before

> me.'" And of His fullness we have all received, and grace for grace. For the law was given through Moses, but grace and truth came through Jesus Christ. No one has seen God at any time. The only begotten Son, who is in the bosom of the Father, He has declared Him. (John 1:1-18)

Read John 1 carefully and notice how John systematically builds a clear and compelling case for the nature and character of Jesus.

- The Word is eternal (John 1:1-2).
- The Word is God (John 1:1).
- The Word is the Creator (John 1:3).
- The Word is the source of life (John 1:4).
- The Word is the source of salvation (John 1:12).
- The Word became flesh (John 1:14).
- The Word is the Son of God sent by the Father (John 1:14).

Rather than giving a detailed account of the birth of Jesus, John, in his own style, writes an explicit description of *who* Jesus is.

Did you notice, too, that John actually does include the essence of the Christmas story in his introduction?

- The Word is Jesus. Jesus is God incarnate. Jesus came into the world that He created to live among His people (John 1:10, 14).
- Jesus is the Lamb of God who takes away the sin of the world (John 1:29, 36), the Son of God (John 1:34, 49), the King of Israel (John 1:49), the Son of man (John 1:51), and the Messiah (John 1:41).

Jesus, the Creator, stooped to enter His creation. In the first 12 chapters of John's gospel, we read the story of Jesus' earthly ministry, but with a primary focus on His deity and the reason why Jesus became flesh and dwelt among us.

The power and purposes of Jesus the Creator become evident as John describes His earthly ministry, particularly as he details the many miracles Jesus performed. John himself declared, "And there are also many other things that Jesus did, which if they were written one by one, I suppose that even the world itself could not contain the books that would be written" (John 21:25).

Just how many miracles did Jesus perform while on earth? So many that no one but God knows. However, John chose to record just *seven* miracles to make his case for Jesus, the Son of God.

John's selection of these miracles is intentional. To validate the message of Jesus, John purposefully and strategically records (under inspiration of the Holy Spirit) these seven specific "signs" or miracles. They are unique in emphasis and in message. And these are *creation* miracles—*ex nihilo* ("from nothing") miracles—extraordinary supernatural demonstrations that validate Jesus' role as Creator. They give testimony to Jesus' identity as the Son of God, the Messiah, the source of eternal life, the Savior *and* the Creator (John 1:1-3). All seven of these supernatural creation events—creating something from nothing—were accomplished merely by the thought or command of the Creator.

John records these specific creation miracles so we could witness the divine nature of our Lord—the deity of Jesus, as Creator and Savior. They were "written that you may believe that Jesus is the Christ, the Son of God, and that believing you may have life in His name" (John 20:31; see also John 2:11, 23; 3:2; 4:48, 53-54; 6:2, 14; 7:31; 11:47-48; 12:11, 18).

This book will present how each miracle highlighted in John's gospel demonstrates Jesus' authority over all of creation (the physical, chemical, material, and natural universe), His power over life and death as the Son of God, and the spiritual truths taught through His encounter with human need that can and should impact our lives today.

J

Jesus Turns Water into Wine

On the third day there was a wedding in Cana of Galilee, and the mother of Jesus was there. Now both Jesus and His disciples were invited to the wedding. And when they ran out of wine, the mother of Jesus said to Him, "They have no wine." Jesus said to her, "Woman, what does your concern have to do with Me? My hour has not yet come." His mother said to the servants, "Whatever He says to you, do it." Now there were set there six waterpots of stone, according to the manner of purification of the Jews, containing twenty or thirty gallons apiece. Jesus said to them, "Fill the waterpots with water." And they filled them up to the brim. And He said to them, "Draw some out now, and take it to the master of the feast." And they took it. When the master of the feast had tasted the water that was made wine, and did not know where it came from (but the servants who had drawn the water knew), the master of the feast called the bridegroom. And he said to him, "Every man at the beginning sets out the good wine, and when the guests have well drunk, then the inferior. You have kept the good wine until now!" This beginning of signs Jesus did in Cana of Galilee, and manifested His glory; and His disciples believed in Him. (John 2:1-11)

Very little about Jesus' childhood or early adult life has been recorded in the Bible. Mary and Joseph had been told by the angel who Jesus would be, but there is nothing to indicate that Jesus ever revealed His messianic identity during His early years. Even His brothers were unaware of who Jesus really was (John 7:5). But that would all change at the end of the first week of Jesus' public ministry.

While attending a wedding in Cana with His mother and disciples, Jesus learned from Mary that the wedding party had run out of wine. So Jesus told the servants to fill six large stone jars with water. Once filled, He instructed them to draw some out and take it to the master of the feast. Then, when the master of the feast tasted the liquid, it was no longer water, but wine—really good wine. Jesus had instantly created wine out of water.

What Actually Happened?

Chemistry is not a favorite subject of many, but a simple review of the basics shows that even chemistry operates by God's design.

Essentially all of creation is composed of just 94 naturally existing elements. A chemical compound is formed by the binding of elements as a result of a chemical reaction. Chemical compounds can display characteristics completely different from the characteristics of the elements of which they are composed. Only slight differences in chemical structure and composition can yield drastic differences in chemical properties.

Consider the difference between water (H_2O) and hydrogen peroxide (H_2O_2), a difference of just one atom of oxygen. Interestingly, both of these liquid compounds are composed of elements that exist as gases at room temperature. And even at low levels, the difference between the effects of carbon dioxide (CO_2) and carbon monoxide (CO) on human health is drastic—one has little effect on the human body, while the other is deadly!

However, the formation of chemical compounds is not a random process. Their formation is largely controlled by the number of *valence electrons* that an atom has. Elements are arranged on the Periodic Table by group. Elements within the same group generally have the same number of electrons in the outermost electron shell (valence electrons). The arrangement of the Periodic Table displays order and predictability.[1] Chemistry is highly regulated, controlled, and ordered, showing that chemistry functions just as our Creator designed.

The exact classification of the "wine" at the wedding is unknown. The Greek word *oinos* can apply either to the decayed, fermented liquid that intoxicates (containing alcohol), or simply to the nutritious juice fresh off the grapevine.[2] Regardless of the end product, turning water into grape juice instantaneously would have been an astounding creation miracle. The color of the water was not changed by some trick or illusion. Grape juice is not merely flavored water. What occurred by the power of Jesus was a complete change in the chemical composition of the contents of the stone jars.

Naturally occurring liquid water is the most plentiful compound on the planet. The chemical structure of water is rather simplistic, composed of only two hydrogen atoms and one oxygen atom (H_2O). Grape juice, on the other hand, is quite complex and requires substantial effort to prepare (e.g., harvesting, crushing, destemming, pressing, and juice preparation). Grape juice is a complex mixture of chemicals, consisting of approximately 70 to 80 percent water, 18 to 25 percent carbohydrates (e.g., fructose and glucose), 1 percent organic acids (e.g., malic, tartaric, and citric acid), and trace amounts of phenolics, nitrogenous compounds, vitamins, and minerals.

Jesus did not simply change the appearance of the water. The water in the stone jars did not undergo some sort of reaction that changed the structure of the existing elements, affecting its appearance. Jesus did not just rearrange elements to form new compounds. The end product was composed of numerous new chemical compounds composed of different elements that were not previously present.

Jesus actually created new elements and new compounds. Jesus *created* wine—"good wine"—showing His authority over the chemical elements, the basic building blocks of all of creation.

What Can We Learn?

Turning water into wine was the first sign performed by Jesus to manifest His glory (John 2:11). Interestingly, this miracle was not recorded by any of the other gospel writers. This creation miracle is rich with symbolism that John builds upon throughout his gospel. Jesus is the living water. Wine represents the blood of Jesus shed for the forgiveness of sin. In His farewell discourse, Jesus is described as the true vine in which we must abide if we are to bear fruit.

This public, physical demonstration of power over water and wine is the first "sign" that John recounts to validate Jesus' true nature and identity, revealing His glory as Lord of creation and as the Author of chemistry, having authority over the physical universe and the chemical elements that compose the physical universe. Jesus is the ruler and sustainer of the universe. He preserves, conserves, and upholds all of creation.

> For by Him all things were created that are in heaven and that are on earth, visible and invisible, whether thrones or dominions or principalities or powers. All things were created through Him and for Him. And He is before all things, and in Him all things consist. (Colossians 1:16-17; see also Hebrews 1:2-3)

The wine that Jesus created in Cana, in keeping with everything that Jesus created (Genesis 1), was pronounced "good." Jesus produces only the best.

Taking the most abundant chemical compound on earth[3] and transforming it for the benefit of man communicates His care for us, individually and personally, and demonstrates the unlimited resources at His command. Jesus Christ is the One who, in His sovereignty, provides perfectly for all of our needs.

> "Therefore do not worry, saying, 'What shall we eat?' or 'What shall we drink?' or 'What shall we wear?' For after all these things the Gentiles seek. For your heavenly Father knows that you need all these things. But seek first the kingdom of God and His righteousness, and all these things shall be added to you." (Matthew 6:31-33)

2

Jesus Heals an Official's Son

So Jesus came again to Cana of Galilee where He had made the water wine. And there was a certain nobleman whose son was sick at Capernaum. When he heard that Jesus had come out of Judea into Galilee, he went to Him and implored Him to come down and heal his son, for he was at the point of death. Then Jesus said to him, "Un-

less you people see signs and wonders, you will by no means believe." The nobleman said to Him, "Sir, come down before my child dies!" Jesus said to him, "Go your way; your son lives." So the man believed the word that Jesus spoke to him, and he went his way. And as he was now going down, his servants met him and told him, saying, "Your son lives!" Then he inquired of them the hour when he got better. And they said to him, "Yesterday at the seventh hour the fever left him." So the father knew that it was at the same hour in which Jesus said to him, "Your son lives." And he himself believed, and his whole household. This again is the second sign Jesus did when He had come out of Judea into Galilee. (John 4:46-54)

What would you do if your child was close to death and you couldn't find a doctor to help? A Capernaum official found himself in that very circumstance—his son was sick to "the point of death." This desperate father heard that Jesus was in Galilee, and he went to Him, imploring Him to heal his son. Jesus responded, "Unless you people see signs and wonders, you will by no means believe." The official pleaded with Jesus to come before his child died, but Jesus did not go. He simply answered, "Go your way; your son lives." With that simple statement, the man left. The Bible says "the man believed the word that Jesus spoke to him, and he went his way." On the way home, he met his servants and they told him that the fever left his son at the seventh hour on the previous day, the time Jesus had said to him, "Your son lives."

What Actually Happened?

Science teaches us that fevers can be caused by a number of foreign invaders to the body, including bacteria, viruses, fungi, toxins, and parasites. The Bible does not tell us *why* the fever was present—perhaps the official's son had a serious infection that his body was unable to clear. Whatever the cause, we can be sure that the boy's body was waging an unseen war. In response to infection or injury, the body's immune system is activated. The immune response is an extremely ordered and orchestrated temporal cascade of events involving numerous highly specific cell adhesion molecules, signaling receptors, enzymes, soluble and membrane-bound inflammatory mediators, and intracellular signaling pathways.[4] Research shows that fever increases immune system defense capabilities.[5] The hypothalamus, located in the brain and part of the central nervous system, regulates body temperature. Pyrogens released at the sites of inflammation travel via the bloodstream to the hypothalamus, causing an elevation in the body's temperature.[6]

This battle was not invisible to our Lord, and the complexity of the boy's circumstances was not beyond His reach. Jesus actually performed this creation miracle without even seeing the boy. The illness, invisible to the human eye, was in full view of the Creator of the human body. And He spoke healing from a distance, showing that He has authority over space and time. As Creator, Jesus is not confined or bound by space and time restrictions of this world. He is sovereign and transcendent over these, because He existed prior to their creation and is the One who brought them into existence (Genesis 1:1; Colossians 1:15).

Without meeting the child or hearing a detailed explanation from the boy's father, Jesus diagnosed the illness and treated him instantaneously, perfectly eradicating any biological issues that had caused the sickness. Jesus caused the fever to disappear immediately and health to be restored, displaying His Lordship over the created design of the human nervous and immune systems—His authority over human flesh. This creation miracle demonstrated how the human body responded to the Creator's bidding. Only Jesus, Lord over life, can accomplish such miracles.

What Can We Learn?

Many of Jesus' miracles were accomplished simply through His spoken word, including healing the official's son. "Jesus said to him, 'Go your way; your son lives.' So the man believed the word that Jesus spoke to him, and he went his way" (John 4:50). John follows the healing of the official's son with significant theological truths based on this sign, including Jesus' equality with God and the authority of the Son. John also uses these creation miracles to introduce the blessing of eternal life for those who believe. But central to John's message here is the *word* of Jesus.

Healings all show the authority of Jesus over biological processes because He is Lord of life. All of creation stands under the authority of the word of Jesus. It was through this very word that all things were created. Genesis 1 repeatedly uses the phrase "then God said," emphasizing that all creation was brought into existence by the very word of God. God spoke and it happened! Numerous references in the Bible affirm creation being spoken into existence by God.

> By the word of the LORD the heavens were made....For He spoke, and it was done; He commanded, and it stood fast. (Psalm 33:6, 9)

> Praise the LORD from the heavens...in the heights! Praise Him, all His angels...all His hosts! Praise Him, sun and moon...all you stars of light! Praise Him, you heavens of heavens, And you waters above the heavens! Let them praise the name of the LORD, For He commanded and they were created. (Psalm 148:1-5)

> By faith we understand that the worlds were framed by the word of God, so that the things which are seen were not made of things which are visible. (Hebrews 11:3)

God's spoken word is the premise of all of creation. And since Jesus is the source of all creation, He is sovereign over all. Jesus now is the preserver and conserver of life, upholding all of creation, "for in Him we live and move and have our being" (Acts 17:28).

But can you guess *how* the Bible says that Jesus holds all things together? According to Hebrews 1:3, it is by His word! There is power in the word of Jesus.

> Who being the brightness of His glory and the express image of His person, and upholding all things by the word of His power, when He had by Himself purged our sins, sat down at the right hand of the Majesty on high. (Hebrews 1:3)

Creation miracles were performed (and recorded) to validate the deity of Jesus so that people would believe in Him and receive eternal life. Significantly, this creation miracle was accomplished by the spoken word of Jesus.

There is authority in the word of Jesus. John's proclamation of the authority of the Son is predicated on the word of Jesus—hearing His word (John 5:24) and hearing the voice of the Son of God (John 5:25, 28; see also 5:19-47).

> "Most assuredly, I say to you, he who hears My word and believes in Him who sent Me has everlasting life, and shall not come into judgment, but has passed from death into life....For if you believed Moses, you would believe Me; for he wrote about Me. But if you do not believe his writings, how will you believe My words?" (John 5:24, 46-47)

Jesus challenged the official by saying that unless he saw the sign he would not believe. But after Jesus pronounced healing on his son, the Bible says that the "man believed the word that Jesus spoke to him, and he went his way" (John 4:50). He believed the word prior to seeing the outcome of the miracle.

When God speaks to you, do you believe and proceed? We're often tempted to wait for a "sign" before we believe, just like the people of Jesus' day—and He called them an evil and adulterous generation (Matthew 12:39; 16:4). They rejected the Word of God incarnate.

There is power in Jesus' words (the words of God incarnate), and there is power in the written Word of God (the Bible). John's testimony shows that within God's Word is the message of salvation and the means of sanctification (John 3:16; 17:17). Jesus did provide many signs and wonders to validate His nature, character, and message. However, we are called to put our trust in His abiding Word, not to look for signs and miracles.

Do you believe it and then live it? Do you believe because God has simply spoken, or are you waiting for a miraculous sign in your life?

3

Jesus Heals an Invalid

After this there was a feast of the Jews, and Jesus went up to Jerusalem. Now there is in Jerusalem by the Sheep Gate a pool, which is called in

Hebrew, Bethesda, having five porches. In these lay a great multitude of sick people, blind, lame, paralyzed, waiting for the moving of the water. For an angel went down at a certain time into the pool and stirred up the water; then whoever stepped in first, after the stirring of the water, was made well of whatever disease he had. Now a certain man was there who had an infirmity thirty-eight years. When Jesus saw him lying there, and knew that he already had been in that condition a long time, He said to him, "Do you want to be made well?" The sick man answered Him, "Sir, I have no man to put me into the pool when the water is stirred up; but while I am coming, another steps down before me." Jesus said to him, "Rise, take up your bed and walk." And immediately the man was made well, took up his bed, and walked. And that day was the Sabbath. (John 5:1-9)

According to the Christopher & Dana Reeve Foundation, nearly 1 in 50 people, approximately six million people, live today with paralysis.[7] There are numerous causes of paralysis, including neurological, traumatic, and infectious or autoimmune disorders. Traumatic brain injury and spinal cord injury are the major traumatic causes of paralysis. Neurological causes of paralysis include amyotrophic lateral sclerosis (also called Lou Gehrig's disease), multiple sclerosis, muscular dystrophy, and peripheral neuropathy. Infectious or autoimmune causes of paralysis include Guillain-Barre syndrome, Lyme disease, rheumatoid arthritis, and spondylitis. Other causes of paralysis include spina bifida, spinal tumors, scoliosis, neurofibromatosis, cerebral palsy, polio, spinal tuberculosis, and stroke.[7, 8]

Paralysis is a complete or partial loss of function, especially involving motion or sensation in a part of the body.[9] Paraplegia involves paralysis of the lower half of the body, including both legs. Quadriplegia is defined as paralysis of the arms and the legs. When the human body experiences paralysis, muscle function is lost due to disrupted communication of nerve impulses between the brain and the muscles, communication that is controlled by the peripheral nervous system (sensory nerves) and the central nervous system.[10]

Consider the intricacy and complexity of the body's nervous system. The nervous system is comprised of the brain and spinal cord (central nervous system) and all the neurons in the body (other than those in the brain and spinal cord; peripheral nervous system). The brain's complexity can be "compared to man-made computers in its astounding ability to process, store, and route information."[11] Billions of neurons throughout the body process and transmit electrochemical signals at remarkable speeds, transmitting impulses at speeds of up to 120 meters per second.[12]

Unfortunately, despite living at a time of tremendous medical advances that can bring healing for many diseases and disorders, only a very small percentage of patients with paralysis regain the use of their arms and/or legs. Current medical research into nerve regeneration has yielded ineffective and, at times, undesirable results: "If the [stem] cells can be stimulated at great expense toward a specified tissue type, they often develop tumors. They also suffer from immune system rejection."[13] But research continues with the goal to reverse the devastating effects of paralysis.

What Actually Happened?

With precise detail, John set the scene for the next miraculous encounter of Jesus. A multitude of invalids lay in the five-roofed colonnades of a pool called Bethesda near the Sheep Gate in Jerusalem. John specifically identified one man who had been an invalid for 38 years, and Jesus healed him, saying, "Rise, take up your bed and walk." Instantly, the man was healed, took up his bed, and began to walk.

Despite the nervous system's amazing complexity, Jesus immediately restored function to the paralyzed limbs of this invalid, once again demonstrating His authority over the biological processes of life. The exact nature of the man's ailments is not completely known, but John defines invalids as those who are blind, lame, or paralyzed (John 5:3).

Simply by His command, Jesus restored the health and wellness of a man who was an invalid for nearly four decades. The man was able to *immediately* get up and walk. Christopher Reeve died while waiting for breakthroughs in nerve regeneration research, with the hope of someday walking again. When Jesus healed the paralytic, He accomplished in a split second what Reeve had waited years for and what cutting-edge medical researchers have been unsuccessful in duplicating today. What an amazing display of the power of Jesus' words! What a tremendous testimony to the authority of Jesus over life, demonstrating that He is, indeed, Lord of life.

What Can We Learn?

Through this creation miracle, John emphasizes Jesus' equality with God (see also John 10:31-39). He is the Son of God who gives life (John 1:4; 5:26, 40), and while He can restore physical life, He is also the source of eternal life.

> But Jesus answered them, "My Father has been working until now, and I have been working." Therefore the Jews sought all the more to kill Him, because He not only broke the Sabbath, but also said that God was His Father, making Himself equal with God. (John 5:17-18)

> For as the Father raises the dead and gives life to them, even so the Son gives life to whom He will...."Most assuredly, I say to you, he who hears My word and believes in Him who sent Me has everlasting life, and shall not come into judgment, but has passed from death into life." (John 5:21, 24)

This once-paralyzed man experienced the regeneration of dead nerves and unresponsive muscle tissue in a physical display of Jesus' authority over human anatomy. The man's physical regeneration highlights the work of Jesus Christ in bringing spiritual regeneration to dead souls. The man was restored to be a "new creation" *physically*, but in Christ we become new creations *spiritually*, receiving eternal life through Him.

> Therefore, if anyone is in Christ, he is a new creation; old things have passed away; behold, all things have become new. (2 Corinthians 5:17)

> For in Christ Jesus neither circumcision nor uncircumcision avails anything, but a new creation. (Galatians 6:15)

Jesus showed that He had the power to restore physical life. More importantly, Jesus has the power to transform and change lives spiritually. The spiritually dead can now "walk" in new life. We as new creations in Christ are called to walk in Him, living in a manner worthy of our calling (John 8:12; 12:35; Colossians 1:10; 1 Thessalonians 2:12).

Therefore we were buried with Him through baptism into death, that just as Christ was raised from the dead by the glory of the Father, even so we also should walk in newness of life. (Romans 6:4)

He who says he abides in Him ought himself also to walk just as He walked. (1 John 2:6)

4

Jesus Feeds the Five Thousand

After these things Jesus went over the Sea of Galilee, which is the Sea of Tiberias. Then a great multitude followed Him, because they saw His signs which He performed on those who were diseased. And Jesus went up on the mountain, and there He sat with His disciples. Now the Passover, a feast of the Jews, was near. Then Jesus lifted up His eyes, and seeing a great multitude coming toward Him, He said to Philip, "Where shall we buy bread, that these may eat?" But this He said to test him, for He Himself knew what He would do. Philip answered Him, "Two hundred denarii worth of bread is not sufficient for them, that every one of them may have a little." One of His disciples, Andrew, Simon Peter's brother, said to Him, "There is a lad here who has five barley loaves and two small fish, but what are they among so many?" Then Jesus said, "Make the people sit down." Now there was much grass in the place. So the men sat down, in number about five thousand. And Jesus took the loaves, and when He had given thanks He distributed them to the disciples, and the disciples to those sitting down; and likewise of the fish, as much as they wanted. So when they were filled, He said to His disciples, "Gather up the fragments that remain, so that nothing is lost." Therefore they gathered them up, and filled twelve baskets with the fragments of the five barley loaves which were left over by those who had eaten. Then those men, when they had seen the sign that Jesus did, said, "This is truly the Prophet who is to come into the world." (John 6:1-14)

Several scientific laws govern the "operation" of the physical universe. Many of these universal laws are probably familiar to most people, including the Law of Gravity, the Laws of Motion, and the Laws of Thermodynamics. The First Law of Thermodynamics is a universal law that states that matter and energy cannot be created or destroyed. Both matter and energy can exist in various forms; however, regardless of their form, the total amount of matter and energy does not increase or decrease, but remains the same. Matter can be turned into energy and energy can be turned into matter, but no new matter or energy can be created. Therefore, the First Law of Thermodynamics is also called the Law of Conservation of Energy.[14]

According to John 1:3, "All things were made through Him [Jesus], and without Him nothing was made that was made" (see also Colossians 1:16). All things in our universe came from Jesus, and He is the Creator of all matter and the laws of the universe that govern matter—as He demonstrated in this feeding of the multitude.

What Actually Happened?

This is perhaps the most familiar of Jesus' creation miracles. The miraculous sign of Jesus feeding this multitude is recorded in all four gospels (Matthew 14:13-21; Mark 6:30-44; Luke 9:10-17). According to the account, there were 5,000 men (John 6:10). As many as 20,000 people could have been present, counting women and children.

Andrew told Jesus of a boy who had five barley loaves and two fish. Imagine the scene! Jesus took the loaves and the fish, and when He had given thanks, He began to distribute the food to those who were seated. There was no limit; the people received as much as they wanted. When they were finished eating, the disciples gathered 12 baskets of leftovers. The people who saw this sign said, "This is truly the Prophet who is to come into the world" (John 6:14).

Each gospel writer provides a unique description of this creation miracle. But in each, the "starting material" (number of loaves and fish) and the amount remaining (12 baskets after everyone had fully eaten) are clearly established. In order to feed everyone, more bread and more fish had to be created.

However, this event contradicts the First Law of Thermodynamics. This event is not scientifically possible. It was supernaturally accomplished by Jesus, the One who established the universal laws of nature, in order to provide another proof of His deity. Feeding all these people starting with just five loaves and two fish necessitated the creation of matter. "In this case, Jesus superseded the law of conservation of matter by creating a great amount of bread and meat for the multitude."[15] And here again Jesus demonstrates that He has sovereign authority over the material/physical world (matter and the laws of nature). As the Creator God, He is not bound by the universal laws that govern matter and creation.

What Can We Learn?

The people on the mountainside that day believed Jesus was the Prophet like Moses that God had promised to raise up (John 1:19-21; 7:40; Deuteronomy 18:18). However, they failed to recognize Jesus' deity, even asking Him for a sign and pointing to the manna that their fathers ate in the wilderness (John 6:30-31). The people missed the meaning of the miracle—they missed the message God had for them.

The purpose of this creation miracle was to demonstrate that Jesus is the Son of God and source of eternal life (John 6:27, 29, 40, 47). John uses this encounter to further validate the nature of Jesus and teach a significant theological lesson. Through the physical, Jesus points to the spiritual. Just as manna was the physical bread sent from heaven for nourishment for physical life, Jesus says, "I am the bread of life" (John 6:35, 48, 51); He was sent from heaven as the source of spiritual life—eternal life (John 6:33, 38, 50, 51, 58).

Jesus provided manna in the wilderness for the Israelites, He provided bread for this crowd in Galilee, and He can provide for you in your time of need. Jesus is our *Jehovah Jireh*, the Lord God our Provider. When the obstacle seems insurmountable, remember that Jesus is sovereign over all resources—He meets our needs, providing both physical and spiritual food for His people (Matthew 6:31-33).

5

Jesus Walks on Water

Now when evening came, His disciples went down to the sea, got into the boat, and went over the sea toward Capernaum. And it was already dark, and Jesus had not come to them. Then the sea arose because a great wind was blowing. So when they had rowed about three or four miles, they saw Jesus walking on the sea and drawing near the boat; and they were afraid. But He said to them, "It is I; do not be afraid." Then they willingly received Him into the boat, and immediately the boat was at the land where they were going. (John 6:16-21)

Have you ever watched "water bugs" scurrying on the top of a pond or creek and wondered how they can actually "walk" on water? One common insect that resides on the surfaces of ponds, rivers, and lakes is the water strider. Its legs are covered with thousands of microscopic hairs that contain air-trapping grooves, a physical characteristic that results in increased water resistance. These water-resistant legs are able to displace approximately 300 times their own volume, providing increased buoyancy for the water strider.[16] The water strider's flotation capacity is also dependent on the surface tension and fluid drag (surface forces) of the water. Therefore, insects that are very light do not experience gravitational forces large enough to "break through" the forces of the water's surface tension.[17]

However, under normal circumstances, people cannot walk on water. The gravitational forces pulling the person down through the contact area with the water's surface override the upward force of the water's surface tension.

What Actually Happened?

The miracle of Jesus walking on the water immediately follows the feeding of the five thousand. Matthew and Mark include slightly more elaborate accounts of this creation miracle; both mention Jesus calming the wind, and Matthew records that Peter walked on the water also (Matthew 14; Mark 6).

Compared to Matthew and Mark, John provides a very brief account of this astounding miracle. At various times in His ministry, Jesus showed authority over nature by calming storms (e.g., Matthew 8:23-27). Although John notes that "the sea arose because a great wind was blowing," he does not include Jesus calming the wind and also omits mention of Peter. Instead, John focuses primarily on the impossible feat of walking on water, a clear, visible demonstration of Jesus' authority over the natural world.

Did Jesus really walk on water? Isn't this miracle maybe a little far-fetched? Some speculate that Jesus actually walked on ice or "viscous" water.[18, 19] Some scholars, even biblical scholars, have tried to explain away the miraculous aspects of Scripture, claiming these are events that did not or could not happen. These conclusions are based on their own presuppositions that reject the presence of God. They do not believe the Bible, and their "faith" is based on their own reasoning. But Jesus' ability to accomplish the supernatural is completely grounded upon His identity as Creator.

As Creator God, He is sovereign over that which He made, including the laws of nature, such as the law of gravity and other forces (buoyancy and surface tension) that should have caused Him to immediately sink into the water.

What Can We Learn?

Despite the brevity, two powerful testimonies to the deity of Jesus are included—a supernatural demonstration and a powerful statement. To further emphasize the divine nature of Jesus, John's account focuses on Jesus' response to the frightened disciples. Jesus follows His demonstration of deity through the creation miracle with a statement of His deity.

The English translations record his statement as "It is I" (John 6:20). This is a translation of the Greek phrase *ego eimi.* In other contexts, including many places in the gospel of John, this is rendered "I AM."

This is a powerful statement, relating His identity to the direct reference of God's self-identification in Exodus 3:14 ("I AM WHO I AM"). The intentionality is evident in John 8. When Jesus is questioned about His identity (John 8:53), He claims equality with the Father, stating, "Most assuredly, I say to you, before Abraham was, I AM" (John 8:58). The Jews knew that He was claiming to be the God who appeared to Moses. Because of this "they took up stones to throw at Him" (John 8:59).

> Of course, if He was not God, what He said *was* blasphemous, which was a capital crime under the Mosaic law (Leviticus 24:16). He was actually claiming to be the God to whom Moses spoke at the burning bush, when he asked God what His name was. God had answered that His name was "I AM" (Exodus 3:14)—that is, He is the God who is eternally self-existent, transcendent to time as well as to space and matter. And *that* was who Jesus was claiming to be![20]

Regardless of the intentionality to point back to the Old Testament, John uses this phrase as a powerful testimony of the nature and character of Jesus' deity. John emphasizes Jesus' deity as the Son of God and the Messiah by including seven "I AM" statements of Jesus:

- I am the bread of life (John 6:35, 48, 51).
- I am the light of the world (John 8:12; 9:5).
- I am the door of the sheep (John 10:7, 9).
- I am the good shepherd (John 10:11, 14).
- I am the resurrection and the life (John 11:25).
- I am the way, the truth, and the life (John 14:6).
- I am the true vine (John 15:1).

Jesus' sovereign authority over the physical universe was demonstrated time and time again through these creation miracles. From this demonstration of divinity proceeds a proclamation of deity, showing He is not only the provider of physical needs, but He is also the provider of our spiritual needs.

Creation miracles validate Jesus' claims to deity. However, His statements are either blasphemy or truth. The "I AM" statements are clear claims of who Jesus is—God Himself. He is who He claims to be, and He demonstrated it with remarkable displays over the physical universe.

As Jesus performed so many remarkable creation miracles, the crowds, the Jewish leaders, and even the disciples acknowledged Him as Rabbi and Prophet. Even today, many accept Jesus as a great teacher or prophet of God. These signs validate His message. And His message cannot be made clearer than when He says, "I AM." He is the Son of God and the only source of eternal life. C. S. Lewis observed that any other view is not possible:

> I am trying here to prevent anyone saying the really foolish thing that people often say about Him: "I'm ready to accept Jesus as a great moral teacher, but I don't accept His claim to be God." That is the one thing we must not say. A man who was merely a man and said the sort of things Jesus said would not be a great moral teacher. He would either be a lunatic—on the level with the man who says he is a poached egg—or else he would be the Devil of Hell. You must make your choice. Either this man was, and is, the Son of God: or else a madman or something worse. You can shut Him up for a fool, you can spit at Him and kill Him as a demon; or you can fall at His feet and call Him Lord and God. But let us not come with any patronizing nonsense about His being a great human teacher. He has not left that open to us. He did not intend to.[21]

What will you do with the claims of Jesus? Creation miracles affirm Jesus as the Son of God, the Messiah. He is not just a great teacher or a prophet. He is the way, the truth, and the life!

6

Jesus Heals a Man Born Blind

Now as Jesus passed by, He saw a man who was blind from birth. And His disciples asked Him, saying, "Rabbi, who sinned, this man or his parents, that he was born blind?" Jesus answered, "Neither this man nor his parents sinned, but that the works of God should be revealed in him. I must work the works of Him who sent Me while it is day; the night is coming when no one can work. As long as I am in the world, I am the light of the world. When He had said these things, He spat on the ground and made clay with the saliva; and He anointed the eyes of the blind man with the clay. And He said to him, "Go, wash in the pool of Siloam" (which is translated, Sent). So he went and washed, and came back seeing. (John 9:1-7)

The human eye is one of the most complex and intriguing organ systems in the body. Only the brain is considered more complicated. The eye is composed of over two million working parts. Millions of photoreceptors enable the detection of ten million color hues. Moving objects can be followed due to six muscles that precisely move the ocular sphere. And it can process information faster than a supercomputer, sending electrical signals at 300 mph.[22]

The eye is an organ constructed of numerous intricate components, including the lens, iris, cornea, pupil, retina, muscles, veins, and optic nerve. The complexity of just the retina is astounding. The retina is light-sensitive tissue, with black and white vision occurring through millions of rods (75-150 million) and color being visualized through the seven million cones in the retina.[23]

Images are created on the retina, and the resulting nerve impulses are sent to the brain through the optic nerve. This occurs through the coordinated function of nerve cells, synapses, and chemical and electrical events.

The visual cortex in the brain "converts" the transmitted image to a picture with the correct color, depth, and contrast. The eye, optic nerve, and visual cortex in the brain are all distinct systems, but all are required to capture, deliver, and interpret what is seen. "The eye is an amazing instrument, but it does not function alone. Even with visual receptors rapidly sending data along the optic nerve, no mental image will form at all unless the brain is properly equipped to manage the input."[24] The extraordinary complexity of the process of seeing, with cooperating functions between the eye, the nerves, and the brain, shows the intricate design of our Creator.

According to the National Federation of the Blind, 1.3 million people in the United States are blind[25] due to a variety of causes, including age-related diseases (macular degeneration, cataract, and glaucoma), eye disorders, eye injuries, and birth defects.[26] Today, some have regained sight through new medical breakthroughs (e.g., eye transplant or stem cell treatment). Certain forms of blindness are reversible; however, most blindness can never be reversed.

What Actually Happened?

Long before medications, transplants, and stem cell treatment, Jesus healed a man who was born blind. The methodology He chose for this creation miracle might be perplexing, though. It was not through a simple verbal command or just a touch of His hand, but was accomplished through mud!

The disciples questioned whether it was the man's sin or his parent's sin that caused him to be born blind. Jesus affirmed that the man's condition was not due to sin, but instead existed so that the works of God might be displayed in him. Jesus spat on the ground and made mud with His saliva. He placed the mud on the man's eyes and told him to go and wash in the pool of Siloam. When the man did, he came back seeing.

We do not know the cause of this man's blindness. Medical science points to malfunction of the eyes, the nerve transmission, or the brain's ability to receive and interpret the information—whatever the reason, this man's anatomy had failed him.

With just a touch (and some mud, in this case), Jesus restored his sight in a moment, providing the man "new life." Jesus again shows His authority over the biological processes of life, a powerful demonstration that He is Lord of life.

Certainly this was a very non-conventional way to heal the blind man. For this particular creation miracle, why did Jesus choose to utilize mud to bring restoration of his eyesight? Think back to Genesis and the creation account of humanity. It was out of the ground that God created man.

> And the LORD God formed man of the dust of the ground, and breathed into his nostrils the breath of life; and man became a living being. (Genesis 2:7)

The restoration of sight in this manner emphasizes Jesus' sovereignty over creation, as He "re-creates" out of the ground to bring "new life" to the man. In both cases, God is shown as sovereign over the life of man, here requiring the blind man's trust and obedience to "go, wash in the pool of Siloam" in order to be healed.

What Can We Learn?

Although the displays of Jesus' power in the creation miracles are incredible, do not be "blinded" by the physical signs and miss the deep spiritual truths to which they ultimately point. Like the other signs, much theological insight can be gained from this creation miracle.

Immediately prior to the healing, Jesus proclaimed, "I am the light of the world" (John 9:5; also 8:12). John references light, darkness, life, and death numerous times throughout his gospel. Often light is closely tied to sight and life, while darkness is connected with blindness and death.

> In Him was life, and the life was the light of men. And the light shines in the darkness, and the darkness did not comprehend it. That was the true Light which gives light to every man coming into the world. (John 1:4-5, 9)

Jesus restored physical sight, a powerful demonstration as the Son of God. But Jesus also came as light into a dark and sinful world. Jesus is the light of God (who brought the knowledge of God) and the light of salvation. He was light sent from heaven (the radiance of God's glory) to illuminate those living in spiritual blindness (darkness), providing spiritual sight. Jesus is the light that came into the darkness of the world to give life—eternal life.

> The people who walked in darkness Have seen a great light; Those who dwelt in the land of the shadow of death, Upon them a light has shined. (Isaiah 9:2)
>
> I, the Lord, have called You in righteousness, And will hold Your hand; I will keep You and give You as a covenant to the people, As a light to the Gentiles. (Isaiah 42:6)
>
> While you have the light, believe in the light, that you may become sons of light......I have come as a light into the world, that whoever believes in Me should not abide in darkness. (John 12:36, 46)

John provides a stern warning to those who reject this light. Choosing to remain blind in darkness brings judgment (John 3:18-19; 8:12-30; 9:39; 12:44-50).

> He who believes in Him is not condemned; but he who does not believe is condemned already, because he has not believed in the name of the only begotten Son of God. And this is the condemnation, that the light has come into the world, and men loved darkness rather than light, because their deeds were evil. (John 3:18-19)
>
> And Jesus said, "For judgment I have come into this world, that those who do not see may see, and that those who see may be made blind." (John 9:39)

We still live in a world filled with spiritual darkness (blindness). However, now *we* are the ones called to be light to the world (Matthew 5:14; Ephesians 5:8-14), bringing the message of salvation and eternal life to a world in need so that the blind may see!

> But even if our gospel is veiled, it is veiled to those who are perishing, whose minds the god of this age has blinded, who do not believe, lest the light of the gospel of the glory of Christ, who is the image of God, should shine on them. For we do not preach ourselves, but Christ Jesus the Lord, and ourselves your bondservants for Jesus' sake. For it is the

God who commanded light to shine out of darkness, who has shone in our hearts to give the light of the knowledge of the glory of God in the face of Jesus Christ. (2 Corinthians 4:3-6)

7

Jesus Raises Lazarus from the Dead

Now a certain man was sick, Lazarus of Bethany, the town of Mary and her sister Martha. It was that Mary who anointed the Lord with fragrant oil and wiped His feet with her hair, whose brother Lazarus was sick. Therefore the sisters sent to Him, saying, "Lord, behold, he whom You love is sick." When Jesus heard that, He said, "This sickness is not unto death, but for the glory of God, that the Son of God may be glorified through it."...So when Jesus came, He found that he had already been in the tomb four days....Then Jesus, again groaning in Himself, came to the tomb. It was a cave, and a stone lay against it. Jesus said, "Take away the stone." Martha, the sister of him who was dead, said to Him, "Lord, by this time there is a stench, for he has been dead four days." Jesus said to her, "Did I not say to you that if you would believe you would see the glory of God?" Then they took away the stone from the place where the dead man was lying. And Jesus lifted up His eyes and said, "Father, I thank You that You have heard Me. And I know that You always hear Me, but because of the people who are standing by I said this, that they may believe that You sent Me." Now when He had said these things, He cried with a loud voice, "Lazarus, come forth!" And he who had died came out bound hand and foot with graveclothes, and his face was wrapped with a cloth. Jesus said to them, "Loose him, and let him go." (John 11:1-44)

Those who had been with Jesus during His earthly ministry witnessed extraordinary miracles of healing, provision, and protection. The six previous creation miracles that John records established Jesus' authority over the material world and over the complex biological processes of life. These signs were powerful demonstrations that He is indeed Lord of creation and Lord of life. What else could Jesus do to demonstrate His deity and authority as the Son of God and the Messiah?

Lazarus, a dear friend of Jesus, was sick. His sisters, Mary and Martha, sent for Jesus, but He replied: "This sickness is not unto death, but for the glory of God, that the Son of God may be glorified through it." But Jesus stayed in the place where He was for two more days before heading out to Judea with the disciples. When He finally arrived, Lazarus had already been in the tomb for four days!

What Actually Happened?

When Jesus instructed those present to remove the stone in front of the tomb, Martha was hesitant because of the potential odor from the body. Jesus reminded her of His previous words—if she believed, she would see the glory of God. Once the stone was taken away, Jesus lifted up His eyes and prayed to the Father. He then cried out with a loud voice, "Lazarus, come forth!" Lazarus, with his hands and feet bound with linen strips and his face wrapped with a cloth, came out of the tomb alive!

Jesus healed many others during His ministry, but He chose not to heal Lazarus so He could perform an even greater sign. Jesus raised from the dead a man who had been entombed for four days. Other creation miracles affirmed Jesus' authority over creation and life. Now Jesus shows His authority even over death. At the command of Jesus, the dead can live again.

The disciples' "beliefs" stood in stark contrast to the beliefs of Lazarus' sisters. When the disciples found out Lazarus was dead, they did not mention anything to Jesus about intervening in the situation, nor did they indicate any desire to return to Judea. The disciples' actions and comments were dictated by the situation and circumstances; they feared for their lives. In the end, the disciples accompanied Jesus, but in doubt—Thomas said, "Let us also go, that we may die with Him" (John 11:16). They did not expect a miracle.

Mary and Martha knew Jesus had the power to heal, both saying to Him, "Lord, if You had been here, my brother would not have died" (John 11:21, 32). They had seen and believed. Perhaps Jesus raising someone from the dead was not on their radar, either. Maybe they thought at this point there was no hope. However, Martha knew Jesus was capable, and she was expectant of *something*: "But even now I know that whatever You ask of God, God will give You" (John 11:22).

What Can We Learn?

Why did Jesus wait until Lazarus had been dead for four days before bringing him back to life? By the fourth day, rigor mortis would have set in. Martha was concerned about the odor from a decomposing body. Bringing Lazarus to life after four days leaves no room for misrepresentation of the miracle. Jesus did not wake Lazarus up. Jesus did not merely resuscitate Lazarus. Jesus reversed the postmortem processes and effects, "re-creating" a new life from a dead and decomposing body. This miracle was a transformation from death unto life.

Like all the previous creation miracles, the physical visual demonstration ultimately brings awareness to a spiritual reality. John reiterates that the signs are performed so that people may believe in Jesus as the Son of God and the source of eternal life. In the most unexpected way, by raising a dead man, Jesus validates His identity, providing the most compelling reason to believe. Jesus shows He has authority over physical death in order to demonstrate that as the Son of God He has conquered death and is the source of eternal life. He affirms this spiritual truth to Martha through the physical creation miracle.

> Jesus said to her, "I am the resurrection and the life. He who believes in Me, though he may die, he shall live. And whoever lives and believes in Me shall never die. Do you believe this?" She said to Him, "Yes, Lord, I believe that You are the Christ, the Son of God, who is to come into the world." (John 11:25-27)

By the word of Jesus He created life. By the word of Jesus He has authority over death, restoring life. All of creation is under His authority. It's important to note that this sign is only recorded by John and it was the climax of the seven creation miracles. It is an obvious prelude to an even greater sign—Jesus' own death, burial, and resurrection.

Christ Is Risen. He Is Risen Indeed.

John wrote that he recorded the signs of Jesus in his gospel "that *you* may believe that Jesus is the Christ, the Son of God, and that believing *you* may have life in His name" (John 20:31; emphasis added). The seven creation miracles purposefully and strategically demonstrate that Jesus is the Lord of creation, Lord of life, and Lord over death, having authority over the physical universe and the biological processes of life. These physical signs show Jesus' sovereign authority and testify to Jesus as the Son of God, the Messiah.

What else could Jesus have done to validate His claims and His message? Well, actually, Jesus predicted not only His own death, but His resurrection (John 3:14; 8:28; 12:32).

> So the Jews answered and said to Him, "What sign do You show to us, since You do these things?" Jesus answered and said to them, "Destroy this temple, and in three days I will raise it up." Then the Jews said, "It has taken forty-six years to build this temple, and will You raise it up in three days?" But He was speaking of the temple of His body. Therefore, when He had risen from the dead, His disciples remembered that He had said this to them; and they believed the Scripture and the word which Jesus had said. (John 2:18-22)

This would be the ultimate validation of who Jesus is so that they might believe and have eternal life. John presents Jesus' ministry of grace and truth, showing that Jesus came to reveal God the Father, teach with authority, and show the way of salvation. But ultimately, Jesus was born into this world to die, not just to validate His claim as the Son of God, but to become the way of salvation and eternal life (John 10:11, 15, 17-18).

The resurrection is the key to the gospel message:

> And if Christ is not risen, then our preaching is empty and your faith is also empty.... And if Christ is not risen, your faith is futile; you are still in your sins! Then also those who have fallen asleep in Christ have perished. If in this life only we have hope in Christ, we are of all men the most pitiable. (1 Corinthians 15:14-19)

From the beginning of his gospel, John portrays Jesus, not only as eternal God, Creator, and God incarnate, but also as Savior.

> The next day John saw Jesus coming toward him, and said, "Behold! The Lamb of God who takes away the sin of the world!" (John 1:29)

Jesus, sent by the Father, is God's way of salvation. He came from heaven not only to *show* us the way, but to *be* the way. John proclaims and defends boldly that Jesus is the Son of God, the Messiah, and *our* source of salvation and eternal life.

> Jesus said to him, "I am the way, the truth, and the life. No one comes to the Father except through Me." (John 14:6)

Why do we need a Savior?

Just as it was true for John's audience, it is true for us today. We live in darkness, spiritual blindness, and are sinners separated from a holy God. What is the effect of our sin on our relationship with God? To understand this, we must go back to Genesis.

When Adam and Eve sinned against God (the Fall), many ramifications followed (the Curse) that impact us even today. *Shame* entered the world. "Then the eyes of both of them were opened, and they knew that they were naked; and they sewed fig leaves together and made themselves coverings" (Genesis 3:7). At that moment, *guilt* also entered the world. "And they heard the sound of the LORD God walking in the garden in the cool of the day, and Adam and his wife hid themselves from the presence of the LORD God among the trees of the garden" (Genesis 3:8). Additionally, *fear* entered the world due to sin. "So he said, 'I heard Your voice in the garden, and I was afraid because I was naked; and I hid myself'" (Genesis 3:10).

Due to their sin, God pronounced a curse upon the serpent, Adam, Eve, and the whole creation. Because of their sin, they, and subsequently we, would experience physical death. "In the sweat of your face you shall eat bread Till you return to the ground, For out of it you were taken; For dust you are, And to dust you shall return" (Genesis 3:19). And they faced the ultimate price for their sin—spiritual death, as they became separated from God (Genesis 3:22).

> Behold, the LORD's hand is not shortened, That it cannot save; Nor His ear heavy, That it cannot hear. But your iniquities have separated you from your God; And your sins have hidden His face from you, So that He will not hear. (Isaiah 59:1-2)
>
> Therefore, just as through one man sin entered the world, and death through sin, and thus death spread to all men, because all sinned. (Romans 5:12)
>
> For the wages of sin is death, but the gift of God is eternal life in Christ Jesus our Lord. (Romans 6:23)

Because of our sin, we need redemption. We need a Savior. From the beginning, God had a plan to deal with our sin. At the time of the Fall, God immediately presented His plan for sending a Messiah. Genesis 3:15 says, "And I will put enmity Between you and the woman, And between your seed and her Seed; He shall bruise your head, And you shall bruise His heel." This verse points forward to Jesus. And through Jesus' death, burial, and resurrection, Jesus our Creator became Jesus our Savior, providing redemption and restoration.

> For since by man came death, by Man also came the resurrection of the dead. For as in Adam all die, even so in Christ all shall be made alive. (1 Corinthians 15:21-22)
>
> He does give aid to the seed of Abraham. Therefore, in all things He had to be made like His brethren, that He might be a merciful and faithful High Priest in things pertaining to God, to make propitiation for the sins of the people. For in

> that He Himself has suffered, being tempted, He is able to aid those who are tempted. (Hebrews 2:16-18)
>
> But this Man, after He had offered one sacrifice for sins forever, sat down at the right hand of God....For by one offering He has perfected forever those who are being sanctified. (Hebrews 10:12-14)

How do we overcome the shame, guilt, fear, and death that separate us from God? Through the death, burial, and resurrection of Jesus Christ!

Jesus brings *reconciliation* in the relationship, as honor is restored and shame is overcome.

> Now all things are of God, who has reconciled us to Himself through Jesus Christ. (2 Corinthians 5:18)

Jesus brings *justification* of the guilt, as we are declared righteous (not guilty) before God, having been imputed with Christ's righteousness.

> Therefore, having been justified by faith, we have peace with God through our Lord Jesus Christ. (Romans 5:1)
>
> And therefore "it was accounted to him for righteousness." Now it was not written for his sake alone that it was imputed to him, but also for us. It shall be imputed to us who believe in Him who raised up Jesus our Lord from the dead, who was delivered up because of our offenses, and was raised because of our justification. (Romans 4:22-25)

Jesus is the *propitiation* of our sin, appeasing the wrath of God and conquering our fear.

> In this the love of God was manifested toward us, that God has sent His only begotten Son into the world, that we might live through Him. In this is love, not that we loved God, but that He loved us and sent His Son to be the propitiation for our sins. Beloved, if God so loved us, we also ought to love one another. (1 John 4:9-11)
>
> And He Himself is the propitiation for our sins, and not for ours only but also for the whole world. (1 John 2:2)

Jesus has overcome and conquered death (Hebrews 2:14-15; Romans 6:4; 1 Corinthians 15:3, 14; Revelation 21:4-5), providing us *eternal life* as new creations in Christ.

> Therefore, if anyone is in Christ, he is a new creation; old things have passed away; behold, all things have become new. (2 Corinthians 5:17)
>
> For if when we were enemies we were reconciled to God through the death of His Son, much more, having been reconciled, we shall be saved by His life. And not only that, but we also rejoice in God through our Lord Jesus Christ, through whom we have now received the reconciliation. Therefore, just as through one man sin entered the world, and death through sin, and thus death spread to all men, because all sinned—(For until the law sin was in the world, but sin is not imputed when there is no law. Nevertheless death reigned from Adam to Moses, even over those who had not sinned according to the likeness of the transgression of Adam, who is a type of Him who was to come.... Therefore, as through one man's offense judgment came to all men, resulting in condemnation, even so through one Man's righteous act the free gift came to all men, resulting in justification of life. For as by one man's disobedience many were made sinners, so also by one Man's obedience many will be made righteous....But where sin abounded, grace abounded much more, so that as sin reigned in death, even so grace might reign through righteousness to eternal life through Jesus Christ our Lord. (Romans 5:10-21)

Jesus—Our Creator, Our Savior

John writes to proclaim the deity of Jesus, the eternal Son of God and the Messiah, providing seven astonishing creation miracles to support his claims. However, John begins his gospel in a manner that takes the reader back to Genesis, declaring that Jesus is Creator (John 1:3, 10). The eternal Word was the One who spoke creation into existence simply by stating "Let there be" (Genesis 1). The same One who said "Let there be light" became the light of salvation. John shows that the Word who created was the very Word who took on human flesh to be the Lamb of God who takes away the sin of the world (John 1:29).

It is not possible to separate the doctrine of creation from the doctrine of salvation. The creation of the world and the resurrection of its Creator are two of the greatest miracles of all the ages.[27]

> We need not wonder that so much importance is attached to our Lord's resurrection. It is the seal and memorial stone of the great work of redemption, which He came to do. It is the crowning proof that He has paid the debt He undertook to pay on our behalf, won the battle He fought to deliver us from hell, and is accepted as our guarantee and our substitute by our Father in heaven. Had He never come forth from the prison of the grave, how could we ever have been sure that our ransom had been fully paid (1 Corinthians 15:17)? Had He never risen from His conflict with the last enemy, how could we have felt confident that He has overcome death—and him that had the power of death, that is the devil (Hebrews 2:14)? But thanks be unto God, we are not left in doubt. The Lord Jesus really rose again for our justification.[28]

Both the creation and resurrection were determined in eternity past. Before the foundation of the world, God knew that the Creator would be sent to become Christ our Savior. This was God's plan before He brought time, space, and matter into existence, before man was created, and before man's disobedience. Almighty, omniscient God knew that Jesus, who would be the Creator, would be the promised seed to bring victory over the enemy (Genesis 3:15) and the Lamb of God who would be slain to be our Redeemer.

> Knowing that you were not redeemed with corruptible things, like silver or gold, from your aimless conduct received by tradition from your fathers, but with the precious blood of Christ, as of a lamb without blemish and without spot. He indeed was foreordained before the foundation of the world, but was manifest in these last times for you who through Him believe in God, who raised Him from the

> dead and gave Him glory, so that your faith and hope are in God. (1 Peter 1:18-21)

God's plan of creation *and* redemption was established before the foundation of the world (see also Ephesians 1:1-6; Titus 1:2; and Revelation 13:8). God the Creator became man to take on Himself the sin of the whole world and die as the substitutionary sacrifice, paying the penalty for the guilt of that sin (Romans 3:10-23; 6:23).

Before Genesis 1:1, Jesus our Creator was Jesus our Redeemer. It *had* to be this way. Who else could save us but the One who made us? Only the Author of life can be the source of eternal life. Only the Agent of creation can produce a new creation. Only the Implementer and Pronouncer of the Curse has the power and authority to overcome and conquer death.

> The Creator has imposed the law of decay and death on his whole creation because of the rebellion of its human stewards. Therefore only *he* can defeat death, and this only by paying the redemption price himself, dying for sin and then rising victoriously from the dead. Thus the great miracle of resurrection requires the great prior miracle of supernatural creation.[29]

The Creator of life is the only One who can be the Redeemer of life. Only God can create life; therefore, only God can redeem and save life. The Creator must also be the Redeemer, for there is no other with the power and authority to accomplish our redemption.

Nor is there salvation in any other, for there is no other name under heaven given among men by which we must be saved. (Acts 4:12)

The Lord Jesus Christ created our life, sustains our life, and died and rose again to redeem our life from sin and death.[30]

This is in fact the great truth of Christianity that sets it apart from all world religions.

> Only orthodox biblical Christianity teaches both the supernatural creation of all things by the transcendent yet personal Creator God, and also the substitutionary death and

bodily resurrection of the Creator, the Lord Jesus Christ.[31]

This message is at the heart of the gospel of John. The overarching purpose is to show that Jesus is this Savior—the Son of God, the Messiah, and the source of eternal life. The creation miracles highlighted by the apostle John were to give testimony to and validate Jesus' identity, so that we would *believe* and that by believing we would receive salvation and have eternal life. This was reiterated after each sign and was clearly the motive of John's portrait of Jesus as he recorded very specific aspects of His life and ministry.

> Jesus answered and said to him, "Most assuredly, I say to you, unless one is born again, he cannot see the kingdom of God....And as Moses lifted up the serpent in the wilderness, even so must the Son of Man be lifted up, that whoever believes in Him should not perish but have eternal life. For God so loved the world that He gave His only begotten Son, that whoever believes in Him should not perish but have everlasting life. For God did not send His Son into the world to condemn the world, but that the world through Him might be saved. He who believes in Him is not condemned; but he who does not believe is condemned already, because he has not believed in the name of the only begotten Son of God." (John 3:3, 14-18)

Jesus did many miracles during His earthly ministry, but even eyewitnesses to Jesus' many miracles refused to believe in Him (John 12:37). Skeptics still remain today. As you read the accounts of these creation miracles, be in awe of the power of God, but do not miss the message! It is the message of salvation—the forgiveness of our sins and the offer of eternal life—found only in the death, burial, and resurrection of Jesus Christ, our Creator and Savior. "Blessed are those who have not seen and yet have believed" (John 20:29)!

REFERENCES

1. McCombs, C. A. 2010. *Structure of Matter.* Dallas, TX: Institute for Creation Research, 35.
2. Morris, H. The Very Good Wine. *Days of Praise,* November 25, 2011.
3. Earth's Water Cycle Protects and Provides. Evidence for Creation. Posted on www.icr.org, accessed February 14, 2012.
4. Ley, K., ed. 2001. *Physiology of Inflammation.* New York: Oxford University Press.
5. Mace, T. A. et al. 2011. Differentiation of $CD8^+$ T cells into effector cells is enhanced by physiological range hyperthermia. *Journal of Leukocyte Biology.* 90 (5): 951-962.
6. Nalin, P. What causes a fever? *Scientific American.* Posted on www.scientificamerican.com November 21, 2005, accessed February 10, 2012.
7. Paralysis Facts & Figures. Paralysis Resource Center, Christopher & Dana Reeve Foundation. Posted on www.christopherreeve.org, accessed February 9, 2012.
8. Paralysis Symptoms: Causes. Better Medicine. Posted on www.bettermedicine.com, accessed February 10, 2012.
9. Merriam-Webster, Inc. Posted on www.m-w.com, accessed February 10, 2012.
10. Paralysis Symptoms, Better Medicine.
11. Thomas, B. Brain's Complexity "Is Beyond Anything Imagined." *ICR News.* Posted on www.icr.org January 17, 2011, accessed February 10, 2012.
12. Suzuki, K. 2010. Myelin: A Specialized Membrane for Cell Communication. *Nature Education.* 3 (9): 59.
13. Thomas, B. Embryonic Stem Cells Approved for First Human Trials. *ICR News.* Posted on www.icr.org August 5, 2010, accessed February 13, 2012.
14. McCombs, *Structure of Matter,* 11-13.
15. Morris, H. 2006. *The New Defenders Study Bible.* Nashville, TN: World Publishing, Inc., 1581.
16. Handwerk, B. Hairy Legs Help Bugs Walk on Water. *National Geographic News.* Posted on November 3, 2004, accessed February 13, 2012.
17. Suter, R. How is it possible for insects and spiders to walk on water or walls? *Scientific American.* Posted January 26, 1998, accessed January 30, 2012.
18. Fairhurst, L. Jesus walked on ice, says study led by FSU scientist. Florida State University news release, April 4, 2006.
19. Did Jesus walk on water? Cornflour effect explained. Dedoimedo. Posted on www.dedoimedo.com.
20. Morris, H. 2003. The "I Am's" of Christ. *Acts & Facts.* 32 (4).
21. Lewis, C. S. 1986. *Mere Christianity.* New York: Macmillan Publishing Company, 40-41.
22. Niles, R. Human Eye. Posted on allaboutthejourney.org, accessed February 16, 2012.
23. Richards, L. 1989. *It Couldn't Just Happen.* Nashville, TN: Thomas Nelson, Inc., 139-140.

24. Thomas, B. It Takes More Than Eyes to See. *ICR News.* Posted on www.icr.org June 25, 2009, accessed February 13, 2012. (See also B. Thomas, Eye Optimization in Creation, ICR News, posted November 23, 2010.)

25. Blindness and Low Vision. National Federation of the Blind Fact Sheet. Posted on www.nfb.org, accessed February 13, 2012.

26. National Institutes of Health. Posted on www.nlm.nih.gov September 29, 2011, accessed February 13, 2012.

27. Morris, H. 2000. *The Long War Against God.* Green Forest, AR: Master Books, Inc., 299.

28. Ryle, J. C. 1986. *Expository Thoughts on the Gospels.* Carlisle, PA: Banner of Truth, 403-404.

29. Morris, *Long War Against God*, 299.

30. Morris, H. Christ Our Life. Posted on www.icr.org, accessed February 17, 2012.

31. Morris, *Long War Against God,* 300.

ABOUT THE AUTHOR

Dr. Brad Forlow received his B.S. in Chemical Engineering at Florida Institute of Technology, and his Ph.D. in Chemical Engineering at the University of Oklahoma. For four years he held the post of Assistant Professor of Research at the University of Virginia before working in pharmaceutical research for an additional six years, most recently for Wyeth/Pfizer. In addition to his science training, Dr. Forlow is completing his theological training at Southwestern Baptist Theological Seminary. Dr. Forlow currently serves on the life sciences research team at the Institute for Creation Research in Dallas, Texas, as well as functioning as Associate Science Editor at the Institute. He is married to Dr. Rhonda Forlow, who serves as ICR's K-12 Education Specialist. The Forlows have three children and reside in Dallas. Dr. Forlow is also the author of *Five Evidences for a Global Flood.*